A

BRIEF ACCOUNT

OF

THE MADRIGAL SOCIETY,

FROM ITS INSTITUTION IN 1741, UP TO THE PRESENT
PERIOD.

By THOMAS OLIPHANT, Esq.

Honorary Secretary.

LONDON:

CALKIN AND BUDD,

BOOKSELLERS TO HIS MAJESTY AND THE ROYAL FAMILY,

118, PALL-MALL.

1835.

Price One Shilling.

The Writer of the present Sketch had intended to annex thereto a short Dissertation on Madrigal Music in general from the earliest period; but finding that he could not compress all he wished to say in a sufficiently concise form, has thought it better to reserve the materials collected for some future opportunity.

ACCOUNT

OF THE

MADRIGAL SOCIETY.

THE earliest Minute Book in the library of the MADRI-
GAL SOCIETY is dated 1744, " At the Anchor and Crown,
White Friars, John Immyns, Esq., Monday Night Club:"
but as Sir John (then Mr.) Hawkins, who was elected a
Member in 1748, distinctly states that it was founded in
the year 1741, at the Twelve Bells, in Bride Lane, I think
we cannot have better authority for dating its commencement at that period. I see no ground for supposing that
a specific Society, under that name, had previously existed;
but simply, that Mr. Immyns, who was a member of the
Academy of Ancient Music, (to which the merit belongs
of rescuing from oblivion many valuable works,) had become so thoroughly imbued with the love of the ancient
school of part-writing, that he determined to found a Club
exclusively for the cultivation of such music; indeed, his
devotion to it was so great, that he looked upon Bononcini
and Handel as the greatest corruptors of the science.

In 1745 the Society removed to the Founders' Arms,
Lothbury, where the Rules appear to have been first re-
gularly drawn up, limiting the number of Members to six-
teen, at an admission fee of 8s. and a payment of 3s. per
quarter. From thence, after a short stay, they went to
the Twelve Bells again; and after that, to the Queen's
Arms, in Newgate Street, where was a room large enough

A 2

for their reception, with a convenient recess for a large press that contained their library.

This last removal took place in 1748, when " The Rules for the better Management of the Madrigalian Society" were revised and promulgated, as follows: viz.—

" THAT every one that proposes to become a Member of this Society shall give in his name a fortnight before he shall be capable of being elected.

" That no person shall be admitted into this Society but what shall subscribe for twelve nights at least, according to the rate of the subscription then in being; except such treble voices as the Society shall procure for their assistance.

" In order to preserve the reputation of the Society, as well as the health of the members thereof; it is agreed, that all musical performance shall cease at half an hour after ten o'clock, unless some of the Members shall be cheerfully incited to sing catches, in which case they shall be indulged half an hour longer and no further.

" That unless the Members of this Society shall, on or before the twelfth night of the current subscription, make, or empower some Member to make, a subsequent subscription for twelve nights longer, such Member, so making default, shall be excluded from and no longer be looked upon as a Member of this Society; and if he is thought worthy of being admitted again, must be proposed afresh, as in case of a new Member.

" That every excluded Member that shall apply to be re-elected, shall, upon his re-election, pay all his arrears that have accrued during the time that he so absents himself, according to the rate of the subscription then in being, before he shall be again admitted a Member;

unless the majority of the Members of this Society shall, on account of the circumstances of such re-admitted Member, or some reasonable cause of such Member's absence, think fit to dispense with the payment of such arrears.

" If any Member, being elected President in his turn, shall be absent on that night, he shall forfeit sixpence the next time he comes, on the demand of the President for the time being, or the Member that is next to him on the list.

" If any Member shall borrow any Madrigal or book (wherein any Madrigal is wrote, that is inserted in the list to be sung on the succeeding night, whereby the Society shall be hindered from performing thereof,) and does not return the same before the hour of eight on the night of performance, such Member shall also forfeit sixpence on such demand as before.

" If any President, that has the custody of the key of the library, shall neglect to bring or send it by eight of the clock on the night of the Society's meeting, he shall, for every such neglect, forfeit one shilling, to be demanded as before.

" It having been long observed that the Members being permitted to sup within the hours set apart for music, (a more intellectual pleasure) has created great hindrance and confusion in the performance, and perhaps would by degrees have eat up the whole time of the Society, and frustrated the chief intent of their meeting; the Members of this Society have agreed to preserve an hour and a half each night free from such interruption; and it is hereby ordered, that if any Member shall eat his supper or any part thereof, after half an hour past eight o'clock and before ten o'clock on the night of the Society's meeting, he shall forfeit six pence, to be applied for buying ruled paper for the use of the Society.

" It is hereby agreed, that the performance of the night shall be divided into two acts, with the interval of about half an hour between each act; and that four Madrigals shall be performed, if time will permit, in each act as usual; and that the office of the President for the two nights shall be to lay out the books of such Madrigals as are to be performed those nights, ready for the Members; and also to have the custody of the key of the library and the cash of the Society; and take care of the reckoning that it does not exceed the usual expense of the Club, according to the subscription then in being; and to enter the list of the Members, (marking against the names of those that are absent,) and if any President shall be absent, the next Member on the list that has served the office of President, shall, in such case or until such President's coming, perform his office.

" It is agreed, that every new Member that shall be introduced into this Society, shall pay half-a-guinea over and above his quarter's subscription, towards the charge of the library; and if any new Member desires it, he shall be indulged one quarter before he pays the said half guinea; but he is not to be at liberty to borrow any books till he shall have paid the same."

ADDITIONAL RULES
Agreed to between 1750 *and* 1757.

Item.—" It is ordered that every night each Member, whose turn it will be to serve President that night four weeks, shall appoint the pieces to be performed for the said night just after the second act is over; that every Member may have timely notice what pieces are to be done, and write out, or practise their parts; and in case of such Member being absent from the Society that night of appointment, the next Member in turn upon the list that shall be then present, shall appoint for him; and in case of his refusal or neglect, the next Member in course, and so on round the list.

Item.—" It is ordered that every Member whose turn it is to serve, or who does serve President of this Society, shall be obliged, every time his turn comes to be President, to present to the Society a score and parts of a Madrigal ready for the Members to perform, under the penalty of forfeiting a penny extraordinary to the plate every night until such score and parts be presented.

Item.—" Any gentleman that has been educated in, or does now belong to any cathedral or choir, shall be admitted to visit this Society at his pleasure.

Item.—" No other stranger shall be admitted to visit this Society, unless his place of usual residence is in the country; and if any such stranger shall be introduced by any Member in person, (without which he cannot be admitted,) he shall pay a shilling for his club.

Item.—" Altho' the breach of some or any of these rules may escape the observation or may have avoided the punishment of this Society, yet no member shall be at liberty to draw the same into a precedent, or enforce any argument to excuse any future breach thereof from any former non-observance.

It is ordered, " That any of the Gentlemen of the Academy of Ancient Music be at liberty to visit this Society whenever they think fit, gratis.

It is ordered, " That the President for the time being shall be at liberty to nominate two catches, to be performed on the nights of his Presidentship after the acts are concluded.

" Whereas this Society is become more numerous than usual.—In order that the same may consist of good and useful performing Members, it is agreed, that every person that shall be hereafter proposed for a Member, (except such as belong to any choir in a cathedral, and except such person as shall be vouched for by two or more members of this Society, to be a person capable of singing his part in concert, both in time and in tune), shall, by way of probation, on that day fortnight that he is proposed, between the acts perform his part, in time and tune, in an ancient madrigal for three or four voices, of such as have been used to be sung in this Society; or some two-part song, the same to be sung with double voices, (or two to a part,) such madrigal or song to be chose out of the library by him that shall propose such person for a new Member, and the part given to him to practise; and that for the future all elections of Members shall be by balloting with beans and peas; the beans to be affirmative, and the peas negative; and it shall be necessary for two thirds of the ballots to be in the affirmative before any new Member can be admitted.

" It is agreed, that when the majority of the Members present shall propose to exclude any Member of this Society, it shall be done by way of ballot; and that a fortnight's notice shall be given of such ballot."

The Society met every Wednesday evening; and, in 1749–50, consisted of twenty-one Members, at the increased rate of 4s. 6d. per quarter; the twelfth part of which subscription was allotted for the total expenses of each night, being at the rate of $4\frac{1}{2}d$. per Member. The places of abode of some of these early worthies of our Society, are given in the general list of Members annexed. " Most of them (says Sir John Hawkins) were mechanics; some weavers from Spitalfields, others of various trades and occupations, who were well versed in the practice of psalmody, and who, with a little pains, and the help of the ordinary solmisation, which many of them were very expert in; became soon able to sing almost at sight, a part in an English or even an Italian Madrigal. They also sang catches, rounds, and canons, though not elegantly, yet with a degree of correctness that did justice to the harmony; and, to vary the entertainment, Immyns would sometimes read by way of lecture a chapter from Zarlino*, translated by himself. They were men not less distinguished by their love of vocal harmony, than by the harmless simplicity of their tempers, and by their friendly disposition towards each other."

If we may judge from some of the specimens to be found in the minute-books, many of them were certainly not learned clerks. Yet how great must have been their refinement of mind and taste, when such men could thus meet, after the fatigues of the day, to enjoy (as is well said in the Rules) a more intellectual pleasure than that of eating and drinking! limiting their expenses to a sum that would barely pay for a morsel of bread and cheese, with the accompanying luxuries of a glass of porter and a pipe, which tradition has handed down as being the " *ne plus ultra*" of their refreshments.

In order, however, to indemnify themselves for such great temperance at the ordinary meetings, they were used occasionally to make little trips into the country, as the following extract from the account books will show.

---

* A most elaborate theoretical writer.

Whit Monday, 11th June, 1753.—At the Green Man, on Blackheath.

	£	s.	d.	
Breakfast		6	8	{ Probably for the Managers only.
Dinner	1	14	6	
Wine	2	18	3	
Lemons.. ...		4	0	
Sugar........		2	0	
Beer		3	0	
Tobacco......		1	2	
Servants......		5	0	
	5	14	7	

Fifteen Members and eight friends were present at this gala.

On a previous occasion, Whit Monday 1751, the party proceeded up the river, breakfasting at Wandsor (Wandsworth), dining at Richmond, besides stopping to wet their whistles at Mortlake, as appears by the bill of the day's expenses.

	£	s.	d.
Breakfast at Wandsor		13	6
Dinner and Wine at Richmond..	4	9	0
Barge	2	1	6
Mortlack			11
	7	4	11

The charge of these merry-makings was defrayed by an extra contribution.

In 1756 the quarterage was raised to 6s. 6d.

On the 16th September, 1761, the following minute is on the books :—" The confusion and disorder of the library having this night been taken into consideration, it was unanimously agreed to put it for the future under the care of a librarian, who should be invested not only with the sole right of disposing, delivering, and managing the same; but should also in some degree serve as secretary, by entering all the proper minutes, taking account of the absent Members, discharging the reckoning, and accounting for the same; in consequence of which, Mr. Deeble having accepted of such office, it was agreed that one shilling per night be, for the future, economized out of each night's expenses, towards making him a gratuity of three pounds per annum, the deficiency to be made good to him out of the stock."

On the 15th April, 1764, the Founder of the Society departed this life, at his house in Cold Bath Fields, and on the 20th June following, it was agreed, " That the sum of 5l. 5s. should be taken out of the stock and given to Mrs. Immyns, for a collection of her late husband's books," which were ordered to be immediately deposited in the library of the Society.

The year previous to his death, a very pleasing mark of respect was paid to Mr. Immyns, who appears to have been in a declining state, as will be seen by the following letter addressed to him by the Members.

Sir,
        At a numerous meeting of the Members of the Madrigal Society, I am desired by all the gentlemen present, to assure you how sincerely they are concerned that your present state of health will not permit you to favour them so often with your company, as they are persuaded your inclination would lead you to do: and as they would be glad to give you a testimony of their sense of the great regard they entertain for a Member of your long standing, who has repeatedly given them proofs of your great attachment to their Society; they still desire you would suffer your name to continue at the head of their list; beg you

would accept of being exempted for the time from all offices, fines, and expenses; and still flatter themselves you will favour them with your presence as often as your health will permit.

I am, with very great regard,
Sir,
Your most obedient humble servant,
PETER NOUAILLE.

Queen's Arms, Newgate Street,
21st Sept. 1763.

To JOHN IMMYNS, Esq.
Haberdashers' Hall, Maiden Lane, Wood Street.

Mr. Immyns's reply was as follows:
SIR,

I am very much obliged to the gentlemen for their concern on account of my bad state of health. They are very right in their judgment, that it 's owing entirely to that, I have not been able to follow my inclinations in attending them. The kind request of my name's being continued on the list of the Society, is too agreeable for me to refuse, and promise to do myself the pleasure of waiting on them as oft as my health shall permit, and I can be any ways useful.—For so many favours received from the Society, and for this, my most grateful thanks are due to them in general and every individual Member, to whom severally, and particularly to you, Sir, the best services in my power are due and owing.

I am, Sir,
Your most obedient humble servant,
JOHN IMMYNS.

Lane's Court, Cold Bath Fields,
or Haberdashers' Hall.

To PETER NOUAILLE, Esq.

Nothing worthy of notice seems to have occurred (the Members continuing always about thirty,) until August 1768, when the subscription was raised to eight shillings per quarter, and it was then also agreed to have an entertainment for the Members and their friends once at least in every year.

In 1769 the Society removed to the Feathers Tavern, Cheapside; in 1775 to the King's Arms, Cornhill; and in 1778 they were at the Half Moon, Cheapside; and also at the London Tavern; between which period and 1785 I find no memoranda.

The following will serve as a specimen of the quaint and primitive style in which their most minute transactions were sometimes recorded;—29th September, 1762. "Gave the waiter for his honesty in taking care of the subscription-money left by mistake on the table, 2s."

Sir John Hawkins, who resigned in 1766, states in his History of Music, published some years after, "The Madrigal Society still exists, but in a manner very different from its original institution, and under such circumstances as render its permanency very precarious." Such may have been the case, but the Minute Books show no change in the proceedings of the Society*.

The Records of 1785 show that the entrance fee had been raised to 1l. 1s. and the quarterage to 10s. 6d., besides 2s. for supper on each night of meeting, which had been altered to once a fortnight.

---

* About this time Mr. Hawkins was knighted and had some accession of property, besides being made a magistrate. May not this have had some influence on him? It is too often the way of the world for men to look down on old acquaintances when they themselves are elevated to a higher sphere. His mechanical friends were then perhaps not genteel enough for him.

How long the Society met at the London Tavern, I cannot state; but in April 1792 they were at the King's Head in the Poultry, and moved from thence in May to the Globe, Fleet Street; as appears by a payment of 13s. 2d. for removing the library. For several years about this period there seldom met above seven or eight Members.

The next removal took place in 1795, to the Crown and Anchor; when, " on account of the advance in wine," the charge for supper was raised to 2s. 6d. for Members, 4s. for visitors, and 3s. for professionals. On the 2nd October 1798, I find mention of a dinner festival for which the Members paid 15s., the same that is at present paid for our anniversary. About this time there was occasionally not a sufficient number present to sing a Madrigal complete in all its parts.

The next occurrence of a dinner was in January 1802, when twenty-eight were present, including the singing boys.

A similar feast took place in 1803, and again in 1809; from which time they have been continued annually: in 1809 our present President, Sir John Rogers, made his first appearance as a visitor.

On the 19th November 1811, it was resolved " to give a prize of a silver cup, value ten guineas, for the best Madrigal that shall be approved, in not less than four nor more than six parts, the upper part or parts to be for one or two treble voices. " The character of the composition to be after the manner of the Madrigals by Bennet, Wilbye, Morley, Weelkes, Ward, Marenzio, and others, and each part to contain a certain melody either in figure or imitation; therefore a melody harmonized will be inadmissible."

" The poetry is recommended to be of the pastoral kind, in English, Latin, or Italian."

For this prize fourteen compositions were sent in, out of which six were chosen at the first rehearsal, and from them two were selected for the final ballot, which showed a majority in favour of "Awake, sweet Muse," by Mr. W. Beale. The other one was "Sweet Philomela," composed by Mr. W. Hawes.

Amongst the unsuccessful compositions, "O sing unto my Roundelay," by Mr. S. Wesley, was much admired; indeed, I believe most people are now of opinion that it was the best. These three, and also "Ah me, quoth Venus," by Mr. W. Linley, are still frequently performed at the meetings of the Society.

In 1814 the annual subscription was raised to 3l., and in 1816 the charge for supper, including a pint of wine, was fixed at 6s.; and the President for the evening was requested to see that the regulation quantity of wine was not exceeded.

The Society about this time lost a very old and esteemed Member whom they were unable to keep any longer on its legs: I allude to a harpsicord, which appears to have been bought in 1777 for 25l., and which had accompanied them in their different changes, but which now, alas! was thought not worth removing.

This may appear a very trifling incident, but I notice it to show that it had been the practice to use an instrument along with the voices in part singing; for further proof of which, I need only refer to a resolution of the 29th October 1766, when it was agreed to hire a harpsicord at 15s. per quarter; and to a payment made in January 1753, to Mr. Veck, "for a string to his bass viol, he having lent it to the Society."

The last grand epoch commenced on the 27th September 1821, when the supper meeting which had been the order of the day for eighty years, gave place to a monthly dinner, which has continued to be the regulation up to the present time, and is now held on the third Thursday of each month, from October to July, at the Freemasons' Tavern instead of the Crown and Anchor; the yearly subscription being 4*l.*, with a charge of 7*s.* 6*d.* for dinner.

In 1827, Mr. Groombridge, who had been father of the Society for many years, resigned through ill health; when it was resolved to appoint a perpetual, instead of a monthly, President, in the person of Sir John L. Rogers, Bart., to whose persevering zeal in the cause of music, the Society mainly owe their present flourishing condition. We need only look for proof of the fact to the minutes of the anniversary in 1834, where it will be seen that accounts of that event were deemed worthy of filling columns in the leading newspapers of the day; that peers of the realm and privy councillors; men of peace and men of war; masters in chancery and briefless barristers; whigs and tories, without distinction, joined in chorussing the self-same strains that were chanted in 1741 by the weavers and spinners of Spitalfields.

*** I had nearly omitted to mention that in March 1832, " a silver snuff-box was presented to Mr. William Hawes, the musical director, as a mark of esteem for his valuable and gratuitous services." If being made of gold could have enhanced its value in Mr. Hawes's estimation, his constant attention to the interests of the Society during many years, richly deserved the gift.

MEMBERS OF THE MADRIGAL SOCIETY,

From its Commencement to the present Time.

John Immyns, 1741, died 1764.

Founder of the Society, by profession an attorney. In his younger days he was a great beau, and had been guilty of some indiscretions which proved an effectual bar to his success, and reduced him to the necessity of becoming clerk to an attorney in the city. The change in his circumstances had not the least tendency to damp his spirits; he wrote all day at the desk, and frequently spent the most part of the night in copying music, which he did with amazing expedition and correctness. He had a cracked counter tenor voice, and played upon the flute, the viol da gamba, the violin, and harpsicord; but on none of them well. At the age of forty he must needs learn the lute, but beginning so late was never able to attain to any great proficiency on it. Having a family, he lived for some years in extreme poverty, the reflection on which did not trouble him so much as it did his friends, one of whom obtained for him the situation of lutist of the Chapel Royal, the salary whereof was forty pounds per annum. He used to act as amanuensis to Dr. Pepusch, and also as copyist to the Society; for on the 10th January 1753, an entry is made in the cash-book " Paid Mr. Immyns the remainder of what was due to him for writing out the three and four part books; and on the 4th December 1760, there is a receipt in his hand-writing for 6*l*. 12*s*. 6*d*., the amount of a subscription made by Mr. Hawkins amongst the Members, for a collection of pieces to be wrote for the use of the Society."

Samuel Jeacock, 1744,

Was a baker by trade. He played on several instruments, but mostly the tenor violin, and at the Society usually sung bass; in the choice of his instruments he was very nice, and, when a violin or violoncello did not please him, would, to mend its tone, bake it for a week or two in a bed of saw-dust. He was one of the best ringers and best swimmers of his time, and died to the grief of many, 1749.

Between 1741 and 1751.

W. Potter, Founders' Arms, Lothbury.

W. Hudden, by the Church-yard, Nicholas-lane.

John Veck, near the Monument.

John Gilbert, Tower-hill.

Richard Cleaver, Cornhill.

Pasco Crocker, Lyme-street.

Richard Simpson, at Messrs. Payne, Lothbury.

Lewis Caton, corner of Bacon-street, Swannfield.

John Worgan, Mus. Doc., Millman-street, Bedford-row. An organ player and composer of some celebrity. He wrote many songs for Vauxhall, between 1750 and 1770.

J. Hawkins, Austin-friars. (Afterwards Sir John.) The writer of the well known History of Music.

Jas. Davidson, Tower-hill.

John Stiegler, Dowgate-hill.

Robert Johnson, dyer, near the Three Cranes.

James Latané, at Mr. Bristolls, Devonshire-square.

Daniel Richards, stationer, Holborn-hill.

John Bradshaw, Lloyds.

George Ward, Size-lane.

T. Winsloe, at Yoakly & Co., Bucklersbury.

H. Margerum, Tower-hill.

W. Bush, Amen-corner.

C. Goodwin, Hog-lane, Moorfields.

Peter Goddard, Fleet-street-hill, Bethnal-green.

T. West, near Whitechapel Church.

W. Richards, Maiden-lane, near the Three Cranes.

C. White, Founders' Arms, Lothbury.

Isaac Kemp.

John Holland.

J. Waters.

Henry Deane.

John Newman.

Nath. Burrough.

W. Curtis.

James Green.

James Randall.

Thomas Curtis.

Peter Nouaille.

—— Sells.

J. Gilbert, jun.

R. Radcliffe.

J. Jones.

R. Edes.

—— Marshall.

—— Cope.

W. Bateman Wright.

—— Reynolds.

—— Morgan.

—— Moze.

—— Hayden.

—— Lowe.

—— Perrin.

—— Shaw.

—— Conway.

—— Parry.

—— Boyer.

—— Strickland.

—— Hughes.

—— Cooper.

—— Markworth.
—— Liddlesdale.
—— Taylor.
—— Coward.
—— Worgan, jun.
—— Pemberton.
—— Maverly.
—— Allen.

—— Warmingham.
—— Wheatley.
—— Lloyd.
—— Johns.
—— Sparrow.
—— Maidwell.
—— Phillips.
T. Atwood.

1754.
Samuel Long.
—— Faulkner.

1756.
James Jennings.
James Crumbleholme.
W. Savage.
—— Burgh.

1757.
W. Brooks.
Rev. C. Torriano.
Jon. Battishill, (afterwards
organist of St. Paul's, Co-
vent Garden, and one of
the finest English glee
writers.)

1759.
F. Barsanti.
B. Hatwell.
James Landon.
Robert Peacock.
Thomas Deeble.

1760.
Andrew Royer.
Richard Thornton.
Samuel Bradshaw.
W. Evans.

1762.
Francis Pemberton.
Samuel Smith.
—— Hooker.
E. T. Warren. Editor of the
well-known collection of
glees, catches, &c.
—— Bramner.

1763.
R. Didsbury.

1764.
W. Mawhood.
Richard Clark, (afterwards
alderman).

1765.
Dr. Arne. The composer of
the opera of Artaxerxes.
Mich. Arne, son of the pre-
ceding.
—— Tomkins.
Luffman Atterbury. Com-
poser of the glee "Come
let us all a Maying go."
Capt. Lowes.
Dr. Heineken.

1766.
James Aucott.

W. Selby.
S. Bloomer.
J. Selby.

1767.

R. Mosely.
P. Leveque.
John Davidson.

1768.

—— Hardy.
P. Turquand.
Granville Sharp.

1769.

James Matthias.
James Brant.
W. Platel.
Dr. Bever. A noted collector of old music.
—— Lomas.
—— Cooke.
—— Desanthien.
Theod. Aylward. One of the assistant directors at the Commemoration of Handel, in 1784.

1770.

John Crawley.
W. Bythesea.

1772.

—— Hickey.
—— Marten.
—— Webster.
—— Starkey.
—— Duval.
—— Pepys.

1774.

Joah Bates. Conductor at Handel's Commemoration, 1784.

—— Gastineau.
—— Laprimaudaye.
—— Thornton.
—— Farmer.
—— Demoutier.

1775.

—— Phipps.
—— Chauvett.
Dr. Grant.
—— Osmond.

1776.

—— Thoyts.
—— Halford.
—— Clarmont.
—— Allen.
—— Arnold.
—— Morland.
—— Barnston.
—— Troward.
—— Atkinson.
—— Thackeray.
—— Holden.
—— Lewis.
—— Baker.
—— Briggs.
—— Charmack.

1777.

—— Woodgate.
—— Demontide.
—— Hobler.
—— Vincent.
—— Walkden.
—— Rhodes.
—— Merryman.
—— Read.
—— Chapman.
—— Styles.

1778.

—— Pearce.

21

—— Rivington.
—— Soaper.
W. Sharp.
—— Greenwood.
Dr. Cooke. Organist and master of the Westminster Abbey boys.

1779 to 1785.

—— Brown.
—— Calvert.
Sir R. Kaye.
J. A. Newman, jun.
—— Loyd.
—— Estcourt.
—— Andrews.
—— Paulaine.
—— Salte.
—— Pugh.
—— Fly.
—— Goodwin, jun.

1788.

Stephen Groombridge.
—— Porter.

1791.

—— Jones.
—— Fitzgerald.
—— Horsfall.
—— White.

1793.

James Bartleman. The first English bass singer of his time.
—— Mordaunt.
—— Jackson.

1794.

R. Smith.

1795.

Capt. Cogan.
—— Chamberlain.
—— Fergusson.
† J. P. Street. Librarian and father of the Society.
—— Bazeley.

1796.

—— Foster.
—— Cresswell.

1797.

—— Bayford.
Mich. Rock.

1798.

R. J. S. Stevens. The glee writer, and Gresham lecturer on music.
W. Horsley, B.M. The glee writer, &c.
W. Wilder.
James Fisher.
W. P. Windus.

1799.

G. Harris.
G. Smith.

1800.

James Stow.
—— Polack.

1802.

Reg. Spofforth. The glee writer.
Dr. C. Stanger.
W. Jones.
Robert Cooke. Master of the Westminster Abbey boys.
Rev. J. Parker. A great proportion of the score-

books belonging to the
Society are in his hand-
writing.
John Cotton.
H. Repton.

1803.

H. Moule.
R. Twining.
Rev. R. Webb. Editor of a
collection of Madrigals in
score.
R. Newman.
R. Smith.
James Street.
Rev. —— Hayes.
Thomas Vaughan. Gentle-
man of the Chapel Royal.
Arthur Morris.

1804.

H. Sanford.
Lewis De Betaz.
E. Burden.

1805.

C. Evans. (Hon.Member.)
Gentleman of the Chapel
Royal.
W. Beale.
John Bayley.

1806.

—— Leslie.
Joseph Smith.
Dr. A. W. Callcott. Well
known for his beautiful
glees and songs.

1808.

James Silver.

1809.

Dr. T. Essex.
† W. Hawes. Gentleman of
the Chapel Royal, master
of the boys, and musical
director of the Society.
† W. Linley. Youngest son
of the distinguished com-
poser Mr. Thos. Linley.

1810.

† Henry Robertson.
Gervas Bradbury.

1811.

G. Gwilt.
Augustus Campbell.

1812.

P. S. Munn.
† Joseph Gwilt.

1813.

Thomas Bradbury.
J. Somerset Smith.
W. Hainworth.
Rev. F. Vickery.

1814.

J. S. Hayward.
Orlando Crease.
J. H. Lean.
A. Pellatt.
G. Laing.
G. E. Williams. Organist of
Westminster Abbey.
T. F. Forster.

1816.

John Bull.
W. Hikeman.

1818.

C. J. Lyon.
J. H. Short.
† Edward Bates. Son of Joah Bates before mentioned.
Rev. Osias Linley. A son of Mr. Thos. Linley before mentioned.

1819.

† Sir J. L. Rogers, Bart. (President.)
J. Blackbourne.
W. Bradley.
Tho. Greatorex. Organist of Westminster Abbey.
Dease Barnwell.

1820.

† Richard Taylor.
T. M. Chaplin.
W. J. Sturch.

1823.

Thomas Bell.
Hon. G. O'Callaghan.
Thomas Welsh. Gentleman of the Chapel Royal.

1824.

† J. Capel. (Vice President.)
James Stanger, jun.

1825.

Temple West.
† J. T. Cooper. (Wine Steward.)
E. Taylor. (Hon. Member.)
James Dodson.

1827.

† J. Barwise.

† C. Baumer. (Treasurer.)
—— Moore.
—— Jolly.

1828.

T. C. Harrison.
W. Gavan.
H. Surman, jun.
Rev. E. Cannon.
† Major Gen.Sir A.Barnard.
John Stephens.
Jonathan Nield. Gentleman of the Chapel Royal.
W. Nield.
† Sir George Clerk, Bart.
† Rev. W. J. Hall.

1829.

† P. J. Salomons.
S. Carey.
E. Harrison.
W. Peacock.
E. Fitzwilliam.
J. O. Atkins.

1830.

John Turner.
J. M. Harris.
Timothy Pinto.
Rev. J. T. Bennett.
† J. N. Macleod.
Vincent Novello. The well known organist and editor of the Fitzwilliam Music.
† Thomas Oliphant. (Secretary.)

1831.

† James Bennet.
J. W. Hobbs.
J. Deacon.

† Right Hon. Lord Saltoun.
W. Coles, jun.
† G. Duval.
† J. Calkin.
† C. Hancock.
† H. Hancock.

1832.

† C. Comerford.
† Joseph Dillon.
† G. Cooper, Deputy Organ-
  ist of St. Paul's.
† Lieut.-Col. Hornby.
W. Taylor.

† Thomas Gladstone, M.P.
James Turle. (Hon. Mem-
  ber.) Organist of West-
  minster Abbey.

1833.

† T. Fitzherbert.
† C. S. Packer.
† J. Bond.

1834.

† Riversdale Grenfell.
† John Lord.
† James King.

The names of the Thirty-five Members constituting the Society in the year 1834, are printed with a †.

THE END.

Printed by Richard Taylor, Red Lion Court, Fleet Street.

CPSIA information can be obtained
at www.ICGtesting.com
Printed in the USA
LVRC021630040419
612993LV00005B/22